Guidance and mark schem
mathematics: Year 6

CW00555816

Contents	Page
About this pack	4
• Using the practice papers	4
About the tests	5
Advice for parents and carers	6
• How this pack will help	6
• Tips	6
Advice for children	7
Test coverage	8
Marking and assessing the papers	10
• Interpreting answers	10
Formal written methods	12
National standard in maths	13
Mark scheme: Set A	14
• Paper 1	14
• Paper 2	16
• Paper 3	18
Mark scheme: Set B	21
• Paper 1	21
• Paper 2	23
• Paper 3	26

About this pack

This pack provides you with practice papers to help support children with the Key Stage 2 Mathematics test. The pack consists of this introductory booklet (including mark schemes) and two sample tests covering a wide range of content taken from the Key Stage 2 programme of study.

Using the practice papers

The practice papers in this pack can be used as you would any other practice materials. The children need to be familiar with specific test-focused skills, such as ensuring equipment functions properly, leaving questions if they seem too difficult, working at a suitable pace for the tests and checking through their work.

If you choose to use the papers for revising content rather than practising tests do be aware of the time factor. These tests are short at only 30 or 40 minutes per paper, as they are testing the degree of competence children have.

About the tests

Each maths test has three papers:

- Paper 1: arithmetic – these are context-free calculations. The children have 30 minutes to answer the questions. 40 marks are available.
- Paper 2 and Paper 3: reasoning – these are mathematical reasoning problems both in context and out of context. The children have 40 minutes per paper to answer the questions. 35 marks are available per paper.

The papers should be taken in order and children may have a break between papers. All of the tests broadly increase in difficulty as they progress, and it is not expected that all children will be able to answer all of the questions.

The marks available for each question are shown in the answer booklet next to each question and are also shown next to each answer in the mark scheme.

Advice for parents and carers

How this pack will help

This pack will support your child to get ready for the KS2 National Mathematics Test. It provides valuable practice and help on the responses and content expected of Year 6 children aged 10–11 years.

In the weeks leading up to the National Tests, your child may be given plenty of practice, revision and tips to give them the best possible chance to demonstrate their knowledge and understanding. It is helpful to try to practise outside of school and many children benefit from extra input. This pack will help your child to prepare and build their confidence.

In this pack you will find two mathematics tests. The layout and format of each test closely matches those used in the National Tests so your child will become familiar with what to expect and get used to the style of the tests. In this booklet you will find a comprehensive answer section and guidance about how to mark the questions.

Tips

- Make sure that you allow your child to take the test in a quiet environment where they are not likely to be interrupted or distracted.
- Make sure your child has a flat surface to work on, with plenty of space to spread out and good light.
- Emphasise the importance of reading and re-reading a question.
- These tests are similar to the ones your child will take in May in Year 6 and they therefore give you a good idea of strengths and areas for development. When you have found areas that require some more practice, it is useful to go over these again and practise similar types of question with your child.
- Go through the tests again together, identify any gaps in learning and address any misconceptions or areas of misunderstanding. If you are unsure of anything yourself, then make an appointment to see your child's teacher who will be able to help and advise further.
- Practising little and often will enable your child to build up confidence and skills over a period of time.

Advice for children

- Revise and practice regularly.
- Spend some time each week practising.
- Focus on the areas you are least confident in to get better.
- Get a good night's sleep and eat a healthy breakfast.
- Be on time for school.
- Make sure you have all the things you need.
- Avoid stressful situations before a test
- If a questions asks you to 'Show your method' then there will be marks if you get the method correct even if your answer is wrong.
- Leave out questions you do not understand and come back to them when you have completed those you can do.
- Check that you haven't missed any questions or pages out.
- Try to spend the last five minutes checking your work. Do your answers look about right?
- If you have time to spare and have a few questions unanswered, just have a go – you don't lose marks for trying.

Test coverage

The test content is divided into strands and sub-strands. These are listed, for each question, in a table on the back cover of every test to allow tracking of difficulties. In a small number of cases, where practical equipment such as containers would be required, these aspects are not tested.

Strand	Sub-strand
Number and place value	counting (in multiples)
	read, write, order and compare numbers
	place value; Roman numerals
	identify, represent and estimate; rounding
	negative numbers
	number problems
Addition, subtraction, multiplication and division (calculations)	add/subtract mentally
	add/subtract using written methods
	estimates, use inverses and check
	add/subtract to solve problems
	properties of number (multiples, factors, primes, squares and cubes)
	multiply/divide mentally
	multiply/divide using written methods
	solve problems (commutative, associative, distributive and all four operations)
	order operations
Fractions	recognise, find, write, name and count fractions
	equivalent fractions
	compare and order fractions
	add/subtract fractions
	multiply/divide fractions
	fractions/decimal equivalence
	rounding decimals
	compare and order decimals
	multiply/divide decimals
	solve problems with fractions and decimals
	fractions/decimal/percentage equivalence
	solve problems with percentages

SCHOLASTIC Guidance and mark schemes

Strand	Sub-strand
Ratio and proportion	relative sizes, similarity
	use of percentages for comparison
	scale factors
	unequal sharing and grouping
Algebra	missing number problems expressed in algebra
	simple formulae expressed in words
	generate and describe linear number sequences
	number sentences involving two unknowns
	enumerate all possibilities of combinations of two variables
Measurement	compare, describe and order measures
	estimate, measure and read scales
	money
	telling time, ordering time, duration and units of time
	convert between metric units
	convert metric/imperial
	perimeter, area
	volume
	solve problems (money; length; mass/weight; capacity/volume)
Geometry – properties of shape	recognise and name common shapes
	describe properties and classify shapes
	draw and make shapes and relate 2D and 3D shapes (including nets)
	angles – measuring and properties
	parts of a circle including radius, diameter and circumference
Geometry – position and direction	patterns
	describe position, direction and movement
	coordinates
Statistics	interpret and represent data
	solve problems involving data
	mean average

Marking and assessing the papers

The mark schemes and answers are located towards the end of this booklet.

The mark schemes provide details of correct answers including guidance for questions that have more than one mark.

Interpreting answers

The guidance below should be followed when deciding whether an answer is acceptable or not. As general guidance, answers should be unambiguous.

Problem	Guidance
The answer is equivalent to the one in the mark scheme.	The mark scheme will generally specify which equivalent responses are allowed. If this is not the case, award the mark unless the mark scheme states otherwise. For example: $1\frac{1}{2}$ or 1.5
The answer is correct but the wrong working is shown.	A correct response will always be marked as correct.
The correct response has been crossed (or rubbed) out and not replaced.	Do not award the mark(s) for legible crossed-out answers that have not been replaced or that have been replaced by a further incorrect attempt.
The answer has been worked out correctly but an incorrect answer has been written in the answer box.	Where appropriate follow the guidance in the mark scheme. If no guidance is given then: ● award the mark if the incorrect answer is due to a transcription error ● award the mark if there is extra unnecessary workings which do not contradict work already done ● do not award the mark if there is extra unnecessary workings which do contradict work already done.
More than one answer is given.	If all answers are correct (or a range of answers is given, all of which are correct), the mark will be awarded unless specified otherwise by the mark schemes. If both correct and incorrect responses are given, no mark will be awarded.

Problem	Guidance
There appears to be a misread of numbers affecting the working.	In general, the mark should not be awarded. However, in two-mark questions that have a working mark, award one mark if the working is applied correctly using the misread numbers, provided that the misread numbers are comparable in difficulty to the original numbers. For example, if '243' is misread as '234', both numbers may be regarded as comparable in difficulty.
No answer is given in the expected place, but the correct answer is given elsewhere.	Where an understanding of the question has been shown, award the mark. In particular, where a word or number response is expected, a pupil may meet the requirement by annotating a graph or labelling a diagram elsewhere in the question.

Formal written methods

The following guidance, showing examples of formal written methods, is taken directly from the National Curriculum guidelines. These methods may not be used in all schools and any formal written method, which is the preferred method of the school and which gives the correct answer, should be acceptable.

Long multiplication

24×16 becomes

```
        ²
      2   4
  ×   1   6
  ─────────
  2   4   0
  1   4   4
  ─────────
  3   8   4
```

Answer: 384

124×26 becomes

```
      ¹   ²
  1   2   4
  ×       2   6
  ─────────────
      2   4   8   0
          7   4   4
  ─────────────
  3   2   2   4
      ¹       ¹
```

Answer: 3224

124×26 becomes

```
      ¹   ²
  1   2   4
  ×       2   6
  ─────────────
          7   4   4
      2   4   8   0
  ─────────────
  3   2   2   4
      ¹       ¹
```

Answer: 3224

Short division

$98 \div 7$ becomes

```
      1   4
  7 │ 9 ²8
```

Answer: 14

$432 \div 5$ becomes

```
        8   6  r2
  5 │ 4   3 ³2
```

Answer: 86 remainder 2

$496 \div 11$ becomes

```
          4   5  r1
  11 │ 4   9 ⁵6
```

Answer: $45\frac{1}{11}$

Long division

$432 \div 15$ becomes

```
          2   8  r12
  15 │ 4   3   2
      3   0   0
      ─────────
      1   3   2
      1   2   0
      ─────────
          1   2
```

Answer: 28 remainder 12

$432 \div 15$ becomes

```
          2   8
  15 │ 4   3   2
      3   0   0     15 × 20
      ─────────
      1   3   2
      1   2   0     15 × 8
      ─────────
          1   2
```

$\frac{12}{15} = \frac{4}{5}$

Answer: $28\frac{4}{5}$

$432 \div 15$ becomes

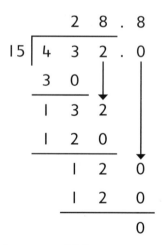

Answer: 28.8

SCHOLASTIC Guidance and mark schemes

National standard in maths

The mark that your child gets in the test paper will be known as the 'raw score' (for example, '62' in 62/110). The raw score will be converted to a scaled score and children achieving a scaled score of 100 or more will achieve the National Standard in that subject. These 'scaled scores' enable results to be reported consistently year-on-year.

The guidance in the table below shows the marks that children need to achieve to reach the National Standard. This should be treated as a guide only, as the number of marks may vary. You can also find up-to-date information about scaled scores on our website: www.scholastic.co.uk/nationaltests

Total mark achieved	Standard
0–59	Has not met the national standard in mathematics for KS2
60–110	Has met the national standard in mathematics for KS2

Mark scheme Set A: Paper 1

Q	Answers	Marks
1	320	1
2	72	1
3	426	1
4	0.89	1
5	60,875	1
6	11,000	1
7	4	1
8	$\frac{3}{7}$	1
9	96	1
10	20	1
11	180	1
12	64	1
13	0.12	1
14	−5	1
15	10,000	1
16	10,755	1
17	2.8	1
18	0.6	1
19	669,000	1
20	2240 Award 1 mark for a correct written method for long multiplication but with one arithmetic error.	2
21	18	1
22	19	1
23	1084	1
24	5750	1
25	23.5 or 23 r8 Award 1 mark for a correct written method for short division but with one arithmetic error.	2
26	$\frac{1}{18}$	1
27	32	1

■SCHOLASTIC Guidance and mark schemes

Q	Answers	Mark
28	279,086 Award 1 mark for a correct written method for long multiplication but with one arithmetic error.	2
29	7400	1
30	$1\frac{3}{8}$	1
31	$18\frac{1}{3}$	1
32	4.85	1
33	54	1
34	45.625 Award 1 mark for a correct written method for short division but with one arithmetic error.	2
35	$\frac{1}{12}$	1
36	2,293,791	1
	Total	**40**

Mark scheme Set A: Paper 2

Q	Answers	Marks
1	$\frac{23}{100}$	1
2	56	1
	16 more blackbirds than robins	1
3	$\begin{array}{r} 6752 \\ +3300 \\ \hline 10052 \end{array}$	1
4	Award 1 mark for a line drawn with a ruler, accurate to within 2mm of centre point and circumference. (Do not reward a mark for line drawn across the full width.)	1
	4cm (Accept any answer between 4.4cm and 4.6cm.)	1
5	396	1
6	Enlarged square should be 9cm on each side. (Only allow 2mm variation for side lengths, and 2 degrees variation for angles.)	1
	81cm² (Units must be given correctly.)	1
7	4425 hours (Accept answer without units, or as a negative number.)	1
	Uranus and Neptune	1
8	$\frac{3}{14}$	1
9	12,364 22,364 **32,364** **42,364** **52,364** 62,364	1
10	718,859 (Accept answer given in words or digits.)	2
	Award one mark for a correct written method but with one arithmetic error.	
11	(Do not award marks for ambiguous answers.)	1

Question 11 matching:

rhombus — Two pairs of parallel sides. Opposite sides of equal length. Opposite angles equal.

parallelogram — Four identical sides. Four identical angles.

trapezium — Two pairs of parallel sides. All sides of identical length. Opposite angles equal.

square — One pair of parallel sides. No sides of equal length.

Q	Answers	Marks
12	$\frac{5}{11}$ $\frac{7}{15}$ $\frac{1}{2}$ $\frac{5}{9}$ $\frac{4}{7}$	1

13

Number of windows	4	5	6	7	8	9	10
Cost (£)	21	25	29	33	37	41	45

Marks: 1

Q	Answers	Marks
14	Award mark only if evidence shows an understanding of the numbers being divisible by 2 (15,322 is even/ends in 2), 5 (13,575 ends in 5) and 3 or 9 (17,253 sum of individual digits).	1
15	26	1
16	8.237 tonnes 1.763 tonnes	1 1
17	$a = 5$, $b = 7$ or $a = 7$, $b = 5$ Do not award a mark if only one combination is given.	1
18	New shape should have the coordinates shown below. All vertices should be accurate to within 2mm. A^1(–6, 1), B^1(–3, 5), C^1(–1, 1) If A^{1}B^{1}C^1 was reflected in the x-axis it would be flipped upside down and all its y co-ordinates would become negative.	1 1 1
19	22p	1
20	Wrong. (643 × 28 = 18,004) Award 1 mark for proof of using an inverse division with the correct method, either 18,104 ÷ 28 or 18,104 ÷ 643.	2
21	$\frac{7}{15}$ 4800	1 1

22

triangles	circles
1	6
2	10
3	14
4	18
5	22

(1 mark for all correct)

$c = 4t + 2$

Marks: 1 / 1

Q	Answers	Marks
23	£10,125 Award 1 mark for a correct method but with one arithmetic error.	2
	Total	**35**

Q	Answers	Marks
1	All sides equal. All sides equal. **Equilateral** Two sides equal. Two angles equal. **Isosceles** One angle equals 90°. **Right-angled** All sides different. All angles different. **Scalene**	1
2	1.3, 3.69, 0.571	1
3	35, 70, 105, **140**, **175**, **210**	1
4	cuboid	1
5	7500	1
6	38°C −3°C Do not award mark for 15°C.	1 1
7	127cm Award 1 mark for either: • the correct approach to converting units but with the wrong answer. or • the correct approach to multiplying a decimal by a whole number but with the wrong answer.	2
8	0.21 — $\frac{1}{6}$ 0.4 — $\frac{2}{5}$ 0.875 — $\frac{7}{8}$ 0.1666 — $\frac{3}{4}$ 0.75 — $\frac{21}{100}$	1

(Note: matching lines are 0.21→$\frac{21}{100}$, 0.4→$\frac{2}{5}$, 0.875→$\frac{7}{8}$, 0.1666→$\frac{1}{6}$, 0.75→$\frac{3}{4}$)

Q	Answers	Marks
9		1

a	0	1	2	3	4	5
b	5	4	3	2	1	0

(Number pairs may be presented in any order.)

Q	Answers	Marks
10	8: eight million 4: forty thousand 3: three hundred	1
11	7cm	1
12	32 £3	2

Q	Answers	Marks
13	$a = 75°$, $b = 105°$	1
	Rhombus. It has all sides the same length, opposite sides parallel, and opposite angles equal.	2
	Award 1 mark for the correct name and two correct facts.	
14	XCIV	1
15	240 children	1
16	50,250	2
	Award 2 marks for a correct answer AND evidence of breaking the larger number into parts, such as $1000 × 50 + 5 × 50$.	
	Award 1 mark for an incorrect answer but with a correct approach to solving the problem and only one arithmetic error.	
17	They each have a medium drink and a biscuit.	2
	Award 1 mark for wrong answers but with working out how much each person spent (£3.04) and evidence of working out different combinations.	
18	21.54cm	1

Q	Answers	Marks

19

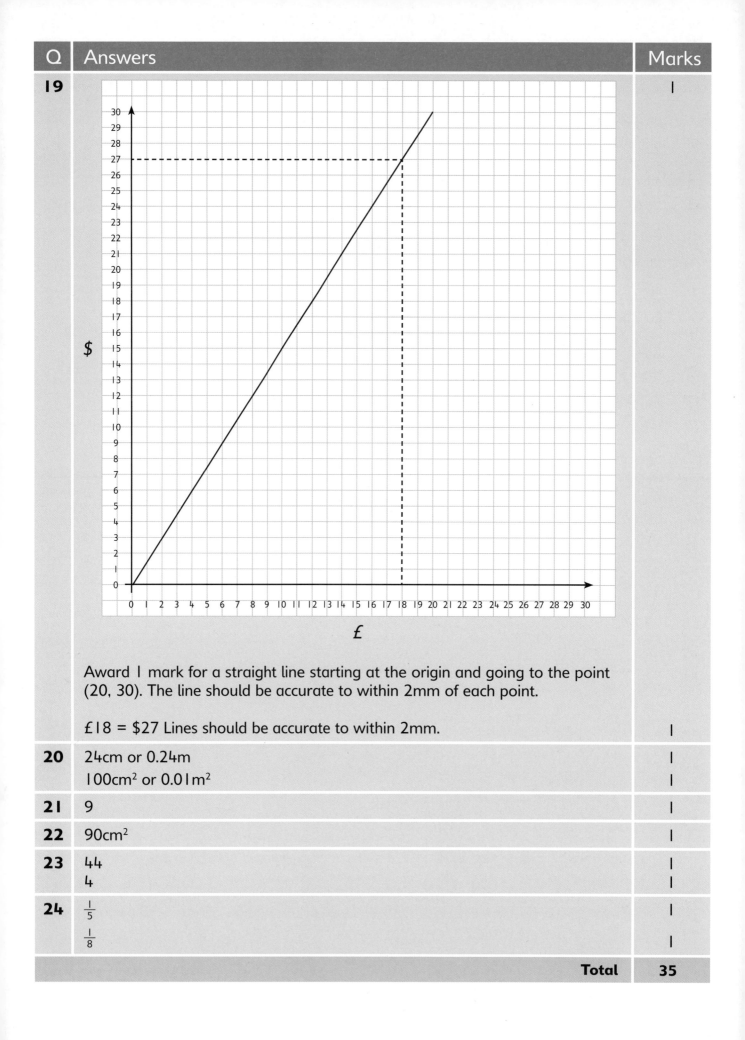

Award 1 mark for a straight line starting at the origin and going to the point (20, 30). The line should be accurate to within 2mm of each point.

£18 = $27 Lines should be accurate to within 2mm.

Marks: 1, 1

Q	Answers	Marks
20	24cm or 0.24m	1
	100cm² or 0.01m²	1
21	9	1
22	90cm²	1
23	44	1
	4	1
24	$\frac{1}{5}$	1
	$\frac{1}{8}$	1
	Total	**35**

Mark scheme Set B: Paper 1

Q	Answers	Marks
1	25	1
2	77	1
3	50	1
4	41	1
5	20,000	1
6	11	1
7	$\frac{3}{5}$	1
8	4.68	1
9	−11	1
10	33,744	1
11	0.1	1
12	2.7	1
13	29,700	1
14	3600	1
15	80	1
16	7.8	1
17	$\frac{1}{4}$	1
18	6281	1
19	$\frac{1}{8}$	1
20	36	1
21	10,750	1
22	489,207	1
23	63	1
24	6.4	1
25	114 Award 1 mark for a correct written method for short division but with one arithmetic error.	2
26	650,000	1
27	$\frac{11}{15}$	1

Q	Answers	Marks
28	216	1
29	28,826 Award 1 mark for a correct written method for long multiplication but with one arithmetic error.	2
30	75	1
31	$\frac{5}{6}$	1
32	150,710 Award 1 mark for a correct written method for long multiplication but with one arithmetic error.	2
33	$2\frac{4}{7}$	1
34	460 r8 or 460.666 or 460.667 or 460 $\frac{2}{3}$ Award 1 mark for a correct written method for short division but with one arithmetic error.	2
35	$7\frac{1}{5}$	1
36	4800	1
	Total	39 40

SCHOLASTIC Guidance and mark schemes

Q.	Answers	Marks
1	$\frac{2}{9}$	1
2	0.8	1
3	5cm 65mm 2000mm 3.5m 400cm	1
4	80g	1
5	$\frac{3}{4}$, $\frac{2}{5}$, $\frac{1}{3}$	1
6	8,406,085 (Accept answer without commas, and with or without spaces between digits.)	1
7	224oz 454kg 35oz	1 1 1
8	8,447,000	1
9	1 in 4 are blue Accept '1 out of 4' or '$\frac{1}{4}$'. 1:2 Accept 1 to 2, but do not award mark for 3:6.	2
10	 Answer should show an understanding that the four angles of a quadrilateral (accept trapezium) add up to 360°.	2
11	In any order: 1 and 96, 2 and 48, 3 and 32, 4 and 24, 6 and 16, 8 and 12 5 and 13	1 1
12	 A square (2, 1)	1 1 1

Q	Answers	Marks
13	£55,175 Award 2 marks for working out: 675 × 45 = 30,375 400 × 62 = 24.800 but an error in addition of them. Award 1 mark for clear demonstration of the correct formal written method for long multiplication but with one arithmetic error.	3
14	 **All sides equal** **All angles equal** rhombus square rectangle parallelogram kite trapezium An equilateral triangle has three identical sides (and all equal angles), whereas an isosceles triangle has only two equal sides (and two equal angles). Award mark if the explanation only covers angles or only covers sides. Do not award marks if angles are defined for one shape, and sides for the other.	1 1
15	$y = 2x + 1$	1
16	140,000	1
17	36cm 48cm^2	1 1
18		1

p	1	3	5	7	9	11	13
q	6	5	4	3	2	1	0

(Number pairs may be presented in any order.)

Q	Answers	Marks
19	60 Award 1 mark for an incorrect answer but with a correct approach to solving the problem and only one arithmetic error.	2

Page 24 of 32

SCHOLASTIC Guidance and mark schemes

Q	Answers	Marks
20		2

Vegetable	Angle	Percentage	People
Broccoli	90°	25	100
Carrots	144°	40	160
Peas	36°	10	40
Spinach	18°	5	20
Cabbage	72°	20	80
Total	360°	100	400

Award 1 mark if at least four rows are correct.

Q	Answers	Marks
21	Adult £4.80, Child £2.50 Award 1 mark for working out the cost of one adult and one child. £9.80 − £17.10 = £7.30	2
	Total	**35**

Mark scheme Set B: Paper 3

Q	Answers	Marks
1	Line must be accurate to 2mm at each end. Square and pentagon. (All must be correct and accurate for 1 mark.)	1
2	0.015 0.051 0.105 0.150 0.501 0.510	1
3	1244 students	1

4

Onions	Potatoes	Carrots
5	10	15
10	**20**	**30**
20	**40**	**60**
100	**200**	**300**

Marks: 1

1:3 (Do not award mark for 5:15.)   1
50%   1

5	$\frac{7}{12}$ $\frac{5}{8}$ $\frac{4}{6}$ $\frac{17}{24}$ $\frac{3}{4}$	1
6	5.5km Award 1 mark for the correct method to find the mean (total divided by the number of days) but with an incorrect answer.	2
7	Answers must make clear that Jim has rounded to the nearest ten thousand, and not to the nearest thousand. 1,248,000	1 1
8	× 1000 ÷ 10 × 10 Award 1 mark if two of the three are correct.	2
9	XI — 9 CX — 11 IX — 90 XC — 110	1

Q	Answers	Marks
10	A¹ should be drawn at (–4, –3), accurate to within 2mm.	I

Q	Answers	Marks
11	12	I

s	I	2	3	10	15	20
c	4	6	8	22	32	42

30

Q	Answers	Marks
11		I
	30	I
12	32p	I
13	15km	I
	30 minutes or $\frac{1}{2}$ hour	I
14	7	I
15	£13.68 Award I mark for the correct conversion of litres to gallons, even if final price calculation is incorrect.	2
16	–3	I
17	£28.75	I
	£2.75	I
	£46	I
18	acute: a = 60° obtuse: b = 120° reflex: c = 300°	I

Q	Answers	Marks
19	360 children Award 1 mark for demonstration of an appropriate method for solving the problem.	2
20	(Award marks if corners accurate to within 2mm.) E = (1, 1), F = (4, 7), G = (10, 4) Award marks if G and F are put the other way around	1 1
21	60m^3 Award 1 mark for evidence of correct method for calculating volume (length × width × height).	2
	Total	**35**

■SCHOLASTIC Guidance and mark schemes

Notes

Notes